LITERATURE FROM CRESCENT MOON PUBLISHING

Sexing Hardy: Thomas Hardy and Feminism
by Margaret Elvy

Thomas Hardy's Jude the Obscure: A Critical Study
by Margaret Elvy

Thomas Hardy's Tess of the d'Urbervilles: A Critical Study
by Margaret Elvy

Stepping Forward: Essays, Lectures and Interviews
by Wolfgang Iser

Andrea Dworkin
by Jeremy Mark Robinson

German Romantic Poetry: Goethe, Novalis, Heine, Holderlin
by Carol Appleby

Cavafy: Anatomy of a Soul
by Matt Crispin

Rilke: Space, Essence and Angels in the Poetry of Rainer Maria Rilke
by B.D. Barnacle

Rimbaud: Arthur Rimbaud and the Magic of Poetry
by Jeremy Mark Robinson

Shakespeare: Love, Poetry and Magic in Shakespeare's Sonnets and Plays
by B.D. Barnacle

Feminism and Shakespeare
by B.D. Barnacle

The Poetry of Landscape in Thomas Hardy
by Jeremy Mark Robinson

D.H. Lawrence: Infinite Sensual Violence
by M.K. Pace

D.H. Lawrence: Symbolic Landscapes
by Jane Foster

The Passion of D.H. Lawrence
by Jeremy Mark Robinson

Walking In Cornwall
by Ursula Le Guin

Languorous Ecstasy:
Selected Poems

LANGUOROUS ECSTASY
SELECTED POEMS

PAUL VERLAINE

Translated by Gertrude Hall
Edited and Introduced by Andrew Jary

CRESCENT MOON

CRESCENT MOON PUBLISHING
P.O. Box 1312, Maidstone
Kent, ME14 5XU
Great Britain
www.crmoon.com

First published 1895. This edition 2017.
© Andrew Jary 2017.

Printed and bound in the U.S.A.
Set in Garamond Book 11 on 14pt.
Designed by Radiance Graphics.

British Library Cataloguing in Publication data

Verlaine, Paul
Languorous Ecstasy: Selected Poems. – (European Poets Series)
I. Title II. Hall, Gertrude III. Jary, Andrew IV. Series
841.8

ISBN-13 9781861712639

Contents

A NOTE ON TEXTS

The poems are taken from *Poems of Paul Verlaine*, translated by Gertrude Hall, published by Stone & Kimball, Chicago, IL, 1895.

In French from *Oeuvres complètes de Paul Verlaine*, published by Vanier, Paris, 1902.

Paul Verlaine by Eugène Carrière

Jean Frédéric Bazille, Paul Verlaine, 1868

Languorous Ecstasy

CLAIR DE LUNE

Votre âme est un paysage choisi
Que vont charmants masques et bergamasques,
Jouant du luth et dansant et quasi
Tristes sous leurs déguisements fantasques.

Tout en chantant sur le mode mineur
L'amour vainqueur et la vie opportune,
Ils n'ont pas l'air de croire à leur bonheur
Et leur chanson se mêle au clair de lune,

Au calme clair de lune triste et beau,
Qui fait rêver les oiseaux dans les arbres
Et sangloter d'extase les jets d'eau,
Les grands jets d'eau sveltes parmi les marbres.

MOONLIGHT

Your soul is as a moonlit landscape fair,
Peopled with maskers delicate and dim,
That play on lutes and dance and have an air
Of being sad in their fantastic trim.

The while they celebrate in minor strain
Triumphant love, effective enterprise,
They have an air of knowing all is vain, –
And through the quiet moonlight their songs rise,

The melancholy moonlight, sweet and lone,
That makes to dream the birds upon the tree,
And in their polished basins of white stone
The fountains tall to sob with ecstasy.

PROLOGUE

Les Sages d'autrefois, qui valaient bien ceux-ci,
Crurent, et c'est un point encor mal éclairci,
Lire au ciel les bonheurs ainsi que les désastres,
Et que chaque âme était liée à l'un des astres.
(On a beaucoup raillé, sans penser que souvent
Le rire est ridicule autant que décevant,
Cette explication du mystère nocturne.)
Or ceux-là qui sont nés sous le signe Saturne,
Fauve planète, chère aux nécromanciens,
Ont entre tous, d'après les grimoires anciens,
Bonne part de malheur et bonne part de bile.
L'Imagination, inquiète et débile,
Vient rendre nul en eux l'effort de la Raison.
Dans leurs veines, le sang, subtil comme un poison,
Brûlant comme une lave, et rare, coule et roule
En grésillant leur triste Idéal qui s'écroule.
Tels les Saturniens doivent souffrir et tels
Mourir, – en admettant que nous soyons mortels. –
Leur plan de vie étant dessiné ligne à ligne
Par la logique d'une Influence maligne.

PROLOGUE

The Sages of old time, well worth our own,
Believed – and it has been disproved by none –
That destinies in Heaven written are,
And every soul depends upon a star.
(Many have mocked, without remembering
That laughter oft is a misguiding thing,
This explanation of night's mystery.)
Now all that born beneath Saturnus be, –
Red planet, to the necromancer dear, –
Inherit, ancient magic-books make clear,
Good share of spleen, good share of wretchedness.
Imagination, wakeful, vigorless,
In them makes the resolves of reason vain.
The blood within them, subtle as a bane,
Burning as lava, scarce, flows ever fraught
With sad ideals that ever come to naught.
Such must Saturnians suffer, such must die, –
If so that death destruction doth imply, –
Their lives being ordered in this dismal sense
By logic of a malign Influence.

NEVERMORE

Souvenir, souvenir, que me veux-tu? L'automne
Faisait voler la grive à travers l'air atone,
Et le soleil dardait un rayon monotone
Sur le bois jaunissant où la bise détone.

Nous étions seul à seule et marchions en rêvant,
Elle et moi, les cheveux et la pensée au vent.
Soudain, tournant vers moi son regard émouvant:
«Quel fut ton plus beau jour!» fit sa voix d'or vivant,

Sa voix douce et sonore, au frais timbre angélique.
Un sourire discret lui donna la réplique,
Et je baisai sa main blanche, dévotement.

– Ah! les premières fleurs qu'elles sont parfumées!
Et qu'il bruit avec un murmure charmant
Le premier oui qui sort de lèvres bien-aimées!

NEVERMORE

Remembrance, what wilt thou with me? The year
Declined; in the still air the thrush piped clear,
The languid sunshine did incurious peer
Among the thinned leaves of the forest sere.

We were alone, and pensively we strolled,
With straying locks and fancies, when, behold
Her turn to let her thrilling gaze enfold,
And ask me in her voice of living gold,

Her fresh young voice, "What was thy happiest day?"
I smiled discreetly for all answer, and
Devotedly I kissed her fair white hand.

– Ah, me! The earliest flowers, how sweet are they!
And in how exquisite a whisper slips
The earliest "Yes" from well-beloved lips!

APRÈS TROIS ANS

Ayant poussé la porte étroite qui chancelle,
Je me suis promené dans le petit jardin
Qu'éclairait doucement le soleil du matin,
Pailletant chaque fleur d'une humide étincelle.

Rien n'a changé. J'ai tout revu: l'humble tonnelle
De vigne folle avec les chaises de rotin...
Le jet d'eau fait toujours son murmure argentin
Et le vieux tremble sa plainte sempiternelle.

Les roses comme avant palpitent; comme avant,
Les grands lys orgueilleux se balancent au vent.
Chaque alouette qui va et vient m'est connue.

Même j'ai retrouvé debout la Velléda,
Dont le plâtre s'écaille au bout de l'avenue.
– Grêle, parmi l'odeur fade du réséda.

AFTER THREE YEARS

When I had pushed the narrow garden-door,
Once more I stood within the green retreat;
Softly the morning sunshine lighted it,
And every flow'r a humid spangle wore.

Nothing is changed. I see it all once more:
The vine-clad arbor with its rustic seat...
The waterjet still plashes silver sweet,
The ancient aspen rustles as of yore.

The roses throb as in a bygone day,
As they were wont, the tall proud lilies sway.
Each bird that lights and twitters is a friend.

I even found the Flora standing yet,
Whose plaster crumbles at the alley's end,
– Slim, 'mid the foolish scent of mignonette.

MON RÊVE FAMILIER

Je fais souvent ce rêve étrange et pénétrant
D'une femme inconnue, et que j'aime, et qui m'aime,
Et qui n'est, chaque fois, ni tout à fait la même
Ni tout à fait une autre, et m'aime et me comprend.

Car elle me comprend, et mon coeur, transparent
Pour elle seule, hélas! cesse d'être un problème
Pour elle seule, et les moiteurs de mon front blême,
Elle seule les sait rafraîchir, en pleurant.

Est-elle brune, blonde ou rousse? – Je l'ignore.
Son nom? Je me souviens qu'il est doux et sonore,
Comme ceux des aimés que la Vie exila.

Son regard est pareil au regard des statues,
Et, pour sa voix, lointaine, et calme, et grave; elle a
L'inflexion des voix chères qui se sont tues.

MY FAMILIAR DREAM

Oft do I dream this strange and penetrating dream:
An unknown woman, whom I love, who loves me well,
Who does not every time quite change, nor yet quite dwell
The same, – and loves me well, and knows me as I am.

For she knows me! My heart, clear as a crystal beam
To her alone, ceases to be inscrutable
To her alone, and she alone knows to dispel
My grief, cooling my brow with her tears' gentle stream.

Is she of favor dark or fair? – I do not know.
Her name? All I remember is that it doth flow
Softly, as do the names of them we loved and lost.

Her eyes are like the statues', – mild and grave and wide;
And for her voice she has as if it were the ghost
Of other voices, – well-loved voices that have died.

À UNE FEMME

À vous ces vers, de par la grâce consolante
De vos grands yeux où rit et pleure un rêve doux,
De par votre âme, pure et toute bonne, à vous
Ces vers du fond de ma détresse violente.

C'est qu'hélas! le hideux cauchemar qui me hante
N'a pas de trêve et va furieux, fou, jaloux,
Se multipliant comme un cortège de loups
Et se pendant après mon sort qu'il ensanglante.

Oh! je souffre, je souffre affreusement, si bien
Que le gémissement premier du premier homme
Chassé d'Éden n'est qu'une églogue au prix du mien!

Et les soucis que vous pouvez avoir sont comme
Des hirondelles sur un ciel d'après-midi,
– Chère, – par un beau jour de septembre attiédi.

TO A WOMAN

To you these lines for the consoling grace
Of your great eyes wherein a soft dream shines,
For your pure soul, all-kind! – to you these lines
From the black deeps of mine unmatched distress.

'Tis that the hideous dream that doth oppress
My soul, alas! its sad prey ne'er resigns,
But like a pack of wolves down mad inclines
Goes gathering heat upon my reddened trace!

I suffer, oh, I suffer cruelly!
So that the first man's cry at Eden lost
Was but an eclogue surely to my cry!

And that the sorrows, Dear, that may have crossed
Your life, are but as swallows light that fly
– Dear! – in a golden warm September sky.

CHANSON D'AUTOMNE

Les sanglots longs
Des violons
   De l'automne
Blessent mon coeur
D'une langueur
   Monotone.

Tout suffocant
Et blême, quand
   Sonne l'heure,
Je me souviens
Des jours anciens
   Et je pleure;

Et je m'en vais
Au vent mauvais
   Qui m'emporte
Deçà, delà,
Pareil à la
   Feuille morte.

SONG OF AUTUMN

Leaf-strewing gales
Utter low wails
    Like violins, –
Till on my soul
Their creeping dole
    Stealthily wins…

Days long gone by!
In such hour, I,
    Choking and pale,
Call you to mind, –
Then like the wind
    Weep I and wail.

And, as by wind
Harsh and unkind,
    Driven by grief,
Go I, here, there,
Recking not where,
    Like the dead leaf.

LE ROSSIGNOL

Comme un vol criard d'oiseaux en émoi,
Tous mes souvenirs s'abattent sur moi,
S'abattent parmi le feuillage jaune
De mon coeur mirant son tronc plié d'aune
Au tain violet de l'eau des Regrets,
Qui mélancoliquement coule auprès,
S'abattent, et puis la rumeur mauvaise
Qu'une brise moite en montant apaise,
S'éteint par degrés dans l'arbre, si bien
Qu'au bout d'un instant on n'entend plus rien,
Plus rien que la voix célébrant l'Absente,
Plus rien que la voix, – ô si languissante! –
De l'oiseau qui fut mon Premier Amour,
Et qui chante encor comme au premier jour;
Et, dans la splendeur triste d'une lune
Se levant blafarde et solennelle, une
Nuit mélancolique et lourde d'été,
Pleine de silence et d'obscurité,
Berce sur l'azur qu'un vent doux effleure
L'arbre qui frissonne et l'oiseau qui pleure.

THE NIGHTINGALE

Like to a swarm of birds, with jarring cries
Descend on me my swarming memories;
Light mid the yellow leaves, that shake and sigh,
Of the bowed alder – that is even I! –
Brooding its shadow in the violet
Unprofitable river of Regret.
They settle screaming – Then the evil sound,
By the moist wind's impatient hushing drowned,
Dies by degrees, till nothing more is heard
Save the lone singing of a single bird,
Save the clear voice – O singer, sweetly done! –
Warbling the praises of the Absent One...
And in the silence of a summer night
Sultry and splendid, by a late moon's light
That sad and sallow peers above the hill,
The humid hushing wind that ranges still
Rocks to a whispered sleepsong languidly
The bird lamenting and the shivering tree.

IL BACIO

Baiser! rose trémière au jardin des caresses!
Vif accompagnement sur le clavier des dents
Des doux refrains qu'Amour chante en les coeurs ardents,
Avec sa voix d'archange aux langueurs charmeresses!

Sonore et gracieux Baiser, divin Baiser!
Volupté non pareille, ivresse inénarrable!
Salut! L'homme, penché sur ta coupe adorable,
S'y grise d'un bonheur qu'il ne sait épuiser.

Comme le vin du Rhin et comme la musique,
Tu consoles et tu berces, et le chagrin
Expire avec la moue en ton pli purpurin…
Qu'un plus grand, Goethe ou Will, te dresse un vers
                                                classique.

Moi, je ne puis, chétif trouvère de Paris,
T'offrir que ce bouquet de strophes enfantines:
Sois bénin et, pour prix, sur les lèvres mutines
D'Une que je connais, Baiser, descends, et ris.

IL BACIO

Kiss! Hollyhock in Love's luxuriant close!
Brisk music played on pearly little keys,
In tempo with the witching melodies
Love in the ardent heart repeating goes.

Sonorous, graceful Kiss, hail! Kiss divine!
Unequalled boon, unutterable bliss!
Man, bent o'er thine enthralling chalice, Kiss,
Grows drunken with a rapture only thine!

Thou comfortest as music does, and wine,
And grief dies smothered in thy purple fold.
Let one greater than I, Kiss, and more bold,
Rear thee a classic, monumental line.

Humble Parisian bard, this infantile
Bouquet of rhymes I tender half in fear...
Be gracious, and in guerdon, on the dear
Red lips of One I know, alight and smile!

SUR L'HERBE

L'abbé divague. – Et toi, marquis,
Tu mets de travers ta perruque.
– Ce vieux vin de Chypre est exquis
Moins, Camargo, que votre nuque.

– Ma flamme... – Do, mi, sol, la, si.
– L'abbé, ta noirceur se dévoile.
– Que je meure, Mesdames, si
Je ne vous décroche une étoile.

– Je voudrais être petit chien!
– Embrassons nos bergères, l'une
Après l'autre. – Messieurs, eh bien?
– Do, mi, sol. – Hé! bonsoir la Lune!

ON THE GRASS

"The abbe rambles." - "You, marquis,
Have put your wig on all awry." -
"This wine of Cyprus kindles me
Less, my Camargo, than your eye!"

"My passion" - "Do, mi, sol, la, si." -
"Abbe, your villany lies bare." -
"Mesdames, I climb up yonder tree
And fetch a star down, I declare."

"Let each kiss his own lady, then
The others." - "Would that I were, too,
A lap-dog!" - "Softly, gentlemen!" -
"Do, mi." - "The moon!" - "Hey, how d'ye do?"

L'ALLÉE

Fardée et peinte comme au temps des bergeries,
Frêle parmi les noeuds énormes de rubans,
Elle passe, sous les ramures assombries,
Dans l'allée où verdit la mousse des vieux bancs,
Avec mille façons et mille afféteries
Qu'on garde d'ordinaire aux perruches chéries.
Sa longue robe à queue est bleue, et l'éventail
Qu'elle froisse en ses doigts fluets aux larges bagues
S'égaie en des sujets érotiques, si vagues
Qu'elle sourit, tout en rêvant, à maint détail.
– Blonde en somme. Le nez mignon avec la bouche
Incarnadine, grasse, et divine d'orgueil
Inconscient. – D'ailleurs plus fine que la mouche
Qui ravive l'éclat un peu niais de l'oeil.

THE LANE

Powdered and rouged as in the sheepcotes' day,
Fragile 'mid her enormous ribbon bows,
Along the shaded alley, where green grows
The moss on the old seats, she wends her way
With mincing graces and affected airs,
Such as more oft a petted parrot wears.
Her long gown with the train is blue; the fan
She spreads between her jewelled fingers slim
Is merry with a love-scene, of so dim
Suggestion, her eyes smile the while they scan.
Blonde; dainty nose; plump, cherry lips, divine
With pride unconscious. – Subtler, certainly,
Than is the mouche there set to underline
The rather foolish brightness of the eye.

À LA PROMENADE

Le ciel si pâle et les arbres si grêles
Semblent sourire à nos costumes clairs
Qui vont flottant légers avec des airs
De nonchalance et des mouvements d'ailes.

Et le vent doux ride l'humble bassin,
Et la lueur du soleil qu'atténue
L'ombre des bas tilleuls de l'avenue
Nous parvient bleue et mourante à dessein.

Trompeurs exquis et coquettes charmantes
Coeurs tendres mais affranchis du serment
Nous devisons délicieusement,
Et les amants lutinent les amantes

De qui la main imperceptible sait
Parfois donner un soufflet qu'on échange
Contre un baiser sur l'extrême phalange
Du petit doigt, et comme la chose est

Immensément excessive et farouche,
On est puni par un regard très sec,
Lequel contraste, au demeurant, avec
La moue assez clémente de la bouche.

STROLLING

The milky sky, the hazy, slender trees,
Seem smiling on the light costumes we wear, –
Our gauzy floating veils that have an air
Of wings, our satins fluttering in the breeze.

And in the marble bowl the ripples gleam,
And through the lindens of the avenue
The sifted golden sun comes to us blue
And dying, like the sunshine of a dream.

Exquisite triflers and deceivers rare,
Tender of heart, but little tied by vows,
Deliciously we dally 'neath the boughs,
And playfully the lovers plague the fair.

Receiving, should they overstep a point,
A buffet from a hand absurdly small,
At which upon a gallant knee they fall
To kiss the little finger's littlest joint.

And as this is a shocking liberty,
A frigid glance rewards the daring swain, –
Not quite o'erbalancing with its disdain
The red mouth's reassuring clemency.

LE FAUNE

Un vieux faune de terre cuite
Rit au centre des boulingrins,
Présageant sans doute une suite
Mauvaise à ces instants sereins

Qui m'ont conduit et t'ont conduite,
Mélancoliques pèlerins,
Jusqu'à cette heure dont la fuite
Tournoie au son des tambourins.

THE FAUN

An ancient terra-cotta Faun,
A laughing note in 'mid the green,
Grins at us from the central lawn,
With secret and sarcastic mien.

It is that he foresees, perchance,
A bad end to the moments dear
That with gay music and light dance
Have led us, pensive pilgrims, here.

MANDOLINE

Les donneurs de sérénades
Et les belles écouteuses
Échangent des propos fades
Sous les ramures chanteuses.

C'est Tircis et c'est Aminte,
Et c'est l'éternel Clitandre,
Et c'est Damis qui pour mainte
Cruelle fait maint vers tendre.

Leurs courtes vestes de soie,
Leurs longues robes à queues,
Leur élégance, leur joie
Et leurs molles ombres bleues,

Tourbillonnent dans l'extase
D'une lune rose et grise,
Et la mandoline jase
Parmi les frissons de brise.

MANDOLIN

The courtly serenaders,
The beauteous listeners,
Sit idling 'neath the branches
A balmy zephyr stirs.

It's Tircis and Aminta,
Clitandre, – ever there! –
Damis, of melting sonnets
To many a frosty fair.

Their trailing flowery dresses,
Their fine beflowered coats,
Their elegance and lightness,
And shadows blue, – all floats

And mingles, – circling, wreathing,
In moonlight opaline,
While through the zephyr's harping
Tinkles the mandoline.

ÉPILOGUE

I

Le soleil, moins ardent, luit clair au ciel moins dense.
Balancés par un vent automnal et berceur,
Les rosiers du jardin s'inclinent en cadence.
L'atmosphère ambiante a des baisers de soeur,

La Nature a quitté pour cette fois son trône
De splendeur, d'ironie et de sérénité:
Clémente, elle descend, par l'ampleur de l'air jaune,
Vers l'homme, son sujet pervers et révolté.

Du pan de son manteau que l'abîme constelle,
Elle daigne essuyer les moiteurs de nos fronts,
Et son âme éternelle et sa forme immortelle
Donnent calme et vigueur à nos coeurs mous et prompts.

Le frais balancement des ramures chenues,
L'horizon élargi plein de vagues chansons,
Tout, jusqu'au vol joyeux des oiseaux et des nues,
Tout aujourd'hui console et délivre. – Pensons.

EPILOGUE

I

The sun, less hot, looks from a sky more clear;
The roses in their sleepy loveliness
Nod to the cradling wind. The atmosphere
Enfolds us with a sister's tenderness.

For once hath Nature left the splendid throne
Of her indifference, and through the mild
Sun-gilded air of Autumn, clement grown,
Descends to man, her proud, revolted child.

She takes, to wipe the tears upon our face,
Her azure mantle sown with many a star;
And her eternal soul, her deathless grace,
Strengthen and calm the weak heart that we are.

The waving of the boughs, the lengthened line
Of the horizon, full of dreamy hues
And scattered songs, all, – sing it, sail, or shine! –
To-day consoles, delivers! – Let us muse.

II

Donc, c'en est fait. Ce livre est clos. Chères Idées
Qui rayiez mon ciel gris de vos ailes de feu
Dont le vent caressait mes tempes obsédées,
Vous pouvez revoler devers l'Infini bleu!

Et toi, Vers qui tintais, et toi, Rime sonore,
Et vous, Rythmes chanteurs, et vous, délicieux
Ressouvenirs, et vous, Rêves, et vous encore,
Images qu'évoquaient mes désirs anxieux,

Il faut nous séparer. Jusqu'aux jours plus propices
Ou nous réunira l'Art, notre maître, adieu,
Adieu, doux compagnons, adieu, charmants complices!
Vous pouvez revoler devers l'Infini bleu.

Aussi bien, nous avons fourni notre carrière
Et le jeune étalon de notre bon plaisir,
Tout affolé qu'il est de sa course première,
A besoin d'un peu d'ombre et de quelque loisir.

– Car toujours nous t'avons fixée, ô Poésie,
Notre astre unique et notre unique passion,
T'ayant seule pour guide et compagne choisie,
Mère, et nous méfiant de l'Inspiration.

II

So, then this book is closed. Dear Fancies mine,
That streaked my grey sky with your wings of light,
And passing fanned my burning brow, benign, –
Return, return to your blue Infinite!

Thou, ringing Rhyme, thou, Verse that smooth didst glide,
Ye, throbbing Rhythms, ye, musical Refrains,
And Memories, and Dreams, and ye beside
Fair Figures called to life with anxious pains,

We needs must part. Until the happier day
When Art, our Lord, his thralls shall re-unite,
Companions sweet, Farewell and Wellaway,
Fly home, ye may, to your blue Infinite!

And true it is, we spared not breath or force,
And our good pleasure, like foaming steed
Blind with the madness of his earliest course,
Of rest within the quiet shade hath need.

– For always have we held thee, Poesy,
To be our Goddess, mighty and august,
Our only passion, – Mother calling thee,
And holding Inspiration in mistrust.

III

Ah! l'Inspiration superbe et souveraine,
L'Égérie aux regards lumineux et profonds,
Le Genium commode et l'Erato soudaine,
L'Ange des vieux tableaux avec des ors au fond,

La Muse, dont la voix est puissante sans doute,
Puisqu'elle fait d'un coup dans les premiers cerveaux,
Comme ces pissenlits dont s'émaille la route,
Pousser tout un jardin de poèmes nouveaux,

La Colombe, le Saint-Esprit, le saint délire,
Les Troubles opportuns, les Transports complaisants,
Gabriel et son luth, Apollon et sa lyre,
Ah! l'Inspiration, on l'invoque à seize ans!

Ce qu'il nous faut à nous, les Suprêmes Poèles
Qui vénérons les Dieux et qui n'y croyons pas,
A nous dont nul rayon n'auréola les têtes,
Dont nulle Béatrix n'a dirigé les pas,

A nous qui ciselons les mots comme des coupes
Et qui faisons des vers émus très froidement,
A nous qu'on ne voit point les soirs aller par groupes
Harmonieux au bord des lacs et nous pàmant,

Ce qu'il nous faut, à nous, c'est, aux lueurs des lampes,
La science conquise et le sommeil dompté,
C'est le front dans les mains du vieux Faust des estampes,
C'est l'Obstination et c'est la Volonté!

III

Ah, Inspiration, splendid, dominant,
Egeria with the lightsome eyes profound,
Sudden Erato, Genius quick to grant,
Old picture Angel of the gilt background,

Muse, – ay, whose voice is powerful indeed,
Since in the first come brain it makes to grow
Thick as some dusty yellow roadside weed,
A gardenful of poems none did sow, –

Dove, Holy Ghost, Delirium, Sacred Fire,
Transporting Passion, – seasonable queen! –
Gabriel and lute, Latona's son and lyre, –
Ah, Inspiration, summoned at sixteen!

What we have need of, we, the Poets True,
That not believe in Gods, and yet revere,
That have no halo, hold no golden clue,
For whom no Beatrix leaves her radiant sphere,

We, that do chisel words like chalices,
And moving verses shape with unmoved mind,
Whom wandering in groups by evening seas,
In musical converse ye scarce shall find, –

What we need is, in midnight hours dim-lit,
Sleep daunted, knowledge earned, – more knowledge still!
Is Faust's brow, of the wood-cuts, sternly knit,
Is stubborn Perseverance, and is Will!

C'est la Volonté sainte, absolue, éternelle,
Cramponnée au projet comme un noble condor
Aux flancs fumants de peur d'un buffle, et d'un coup d'aile
Emportant son trophée à travers les cieux d'or!

Ce qu'il nous faut à nous, c'est l'étude sans trêve,
C'est l'effort inouï, le combat non pareil,
C'est la nuit, l'âpre nuit du travail, d'où se lève
Lentement, lentement, l'Oeuvre, ainsi qu'un soleil!

Libre à nos Inspirés, coeurs qu'une oeillade enflamme.
D'abandonner leur être aux vents comme un bouleau:
Pauvres gens! l'Art n'est pas d'éparpiller son âme:
Est-elle eu marbre, ou non, la Vénus de Milo?

Nous donc, sculptons avec le ciseau des Pensées
Le bloc vierge du Beau, Paros immaculé,
Et faisons-en surgir sous nos mains empressées
Quelque pure statue au péplos étoile,

Afin qu'un jour, frappant de rayons gris et roses
Le chef-d'oeuvre serein, comme un nouveau Memnon
L'Aube-Postérité, fille des Temps moroses,
Fasse dans l'air futur retentir notre nom!

Is Will eternal, holy, absolute, eternal,
That grasps – as doth a noble bird of prey
The steaming flanks of the foredoomed brute, –
Its project, and with it, – skyward, away!

What we need, we, is fixedness intense,
Unequalled effort, strife that shall not cease,
Is night, the bitter night of labor, whence
Arises, sun-like, slow, the Master-piece!

Let our Inspired, hearts by an eye-shot tined,
Sway with the birch-tree to all winds that blow,
Poor things! Art knows not the divided mind –
Speak, Milo's Venus, is she stone or no?

We therefore, carve we with the chisel Thought
The pure block of the Beautiful, and gain
From out the marble cold where it was not,
Some starry-chitoned statue without stain,

That one far day, Posterity, new Morn,
Enkindling with a golden-rosy flame
Our Work, new Memnon, shall to ears unborn
Make quiver in the singing air our name!

ILLUSTRATIONS

Henri Fantin-Latour, The Corner of the Table, 1872,
Musée d'Orsay, Paris

A NOTE ON PAUL VERLAINE

By Andrew Jary

Paul Verlaine (1844-1896) is one of the great 19th century French poets, part of the group that included Charles Baudelaire, Lautréamont, Gérard de Nerval and of course Arthur Rimbaud. Many of Verlaine's most significant poems are collected in this book, and Verlaine emerges as a highly accomplished artist, with a lyrical rhyming style that's wholly his own (and it sounds particularly beautiful in French – Verlaine is tricky to translate).

Paul Verlaine's era was that of Symbolism and Decadence, and the chief poets of Symbolism and Decadence included Verlaine, Charles Baudelaire, Arthur Rimbaud, Gérard de Nerval, Tristan Corbière, Stéphane Mallarmé, Paul Valéry and Lautréamont. The Symbolist and Decadent age is marked by 'gory exoticism', as Mario Praz put it (289), by the æstheticism of 'beauty', opulence and indulgence, mysticism and black magic, the macabre, where the key phrase is from Paul Verlaine: 'Je suis l'Empire à la fin de la décadence', which he wrote in 1885 in a poem entitled (what else?) 'Langueur'.[1] The word, *decadence*, from Verlaine, connotes profuse amounts of eroticism,

---

1 P. Verlaine, 1999, 134.

debauchery, declining state power, Imperialism and 'perversions'.

Like other poets of the Symbolist era – Arthur Rimbaud, Stéphane Mallarmé, Banville – Paul Verlaine can be seen as post-Romantic. Verlaine's poetry (like Symbolism) exhibits many affinities with Romanticism: the pantheism and nature mysticism; the love of occultism, paganism, Hellenism, travel and exotica; the cult of the individual; the social rebellion; the exaltation of solitude; the sense of melancholy; the emphasis on subjective experience; the use of drugs and intoxicants; the urge to go to extremes; the leaning towards infinity, and so on.

Paul Verlaine was an important poet, but was not epoch-forming like Arthur Rimbaud, Victor Hugo or Charles Baudelaire. Verlaine's poetry is marked by a finely-crafted musicality and sense of form, a delicate sensuality, and large doses of Catholic imagery and religious themes.

Paul Verlaine's emphasis in poetry on the form, precision, musicality and beauty of poetry contrasted dramatically with the sense of burning abandon in poets such as Rimbaud, de Nerval and Lautréamont. There is a wildness in Arthur Rimbaud's poetic sensibility that no poetic form can quite contain (despite his use of many traditional forms). While Verlaine's poetry remains firmly within the form of the stanza, Rimbaud's threatens to burst out. What Rimbaud and Verlaine share, with poets such as Baudelaire, William Blake, Novalis and Friedrich Hölderlin, is a belief in the magic of poetry. Theirs is a poetics of the word, an 'alchemy of the word'. as Rimbaud put it.

Paul Verlaine developed Gérard de Nerval's mythopoeic brand of poetry, but for Verlaine form was crucial. 'Music before everything', he wrote in his influential poem 'Art poétique' (1974, 172-3). Verlaine's delicate poetic musicality was highly refined even in his first volume of verse, *Poèmes saturniens*. A poem such as 'Cansons d'automne' displays the finesse of Verlaine's sense of sound and music in poetry (it's also an important poem for France politically):

Les sanglots longs
Des violons
  De l'automne
Blessent mon cœur
D'une langueur
  Monotone.
(The long sobbing of the violins of autumn wounds my heart with a monotonous languour [1974, 44])

VERLAINE AND RIMBAUD

It is significant that the main documents relating to the relationship between Paul Verlaine and Arthur Rimbaud is their poetry.[2] Poetry is a very particular kind of creation, often having an obscure or distant link to the poet's life or experience (involving layers and veils of stylization and mythicization). Consequently, using Verlaine's and Rimbaud's poems of the period or later poetry to find out about their years together is fraught with problems.

Paul Verlaine was ten years older than Arthur Rimbaud. Next to the phenomenally talented teenage poet, Verlaine must have felt inadequate. By an early age Rimbaud had already attained everything that Verlaine had, artistically, and had far surpassed him. The elements of their time together have become famous – the arguments, the dissolute life in Northern Europe (including Paris and London), and the incident with the gun, when Verlaine shot Rimbaud during an argument.

Before he met Paul Verlaine, Arthur Rimbaud admired his poetry. In his 'seer letter' of May 15, 1871, Rimbaud re-writes the history of poetry. It is all junk, he claims, from the Greeks to the Romantics (*Collected Works*, 305). Among the few poets to get a

---

2 W. Fowlie, 1995, 52.

favourable mention by the young Rimbaud are the Parnassians Albert Mérat and Paul Verlaine (ib., 307).

Critics generally portray Paul Verlaine as the weaker, more feminine partner in their homosexual relationship, with Arthur Rimbaud as the more aggressive, more cynical partner. Rimbaud seemed to care much less about the relationship and about himself than Verlaine did. He certainly cared much less about art. It was Verlaine who tried to patch up the relationship after an interval apart. But both men had similar temperaments – too similar; both men were prone to violent mood swings; both were highly individual, self-opinionated, egotistic, unwilling to compromise. They seemed well suited to each other, and yet, as events proved, ultimately incompatible.

Critics turn to Arthur Rimbaud's *A Season in Hell* (1873) as an account of aspects of the Verlaine-Rimbaud relationship: parts of *A Season In Hell* are intense, heartfelt, ashamed, vitriolic, unrepentant, transgressive, chaotic, stupid and sometimes violent. The first 'Delirium' poem is particularly visceral in its imagery, and intense in its self-examination.

Whether or not 'Delirium I: The Foolish Virgin' is an account of Arthur Rimbaud's time with Paul Verlaine, it certainly contains some of Rimbaud's most vivid and tortured poetry. Right from the start of 'Delirium I' the narrator or confessor is talking in extreme terms of being drunk, lost and impure. The confessor says that there has never been 'deliriums and tortures like this'. The confessor says he is really suffering. He speaks of the damned and the dead, of ghosts and murder, of treasure being stained with blood, of skeletons and throats being cut ('it'll be "disgusting"'). The Infernal Bridegroom says he will gash himself up, will make himself ugly, will howl in the streets: '[j]e veux devenir bien fou de rage (I want to become mad with rage)'.[3]

In 'Delirium I', Arthur Rimbaud's poetic voice apparently impersonates that of a 'Foolish Virgin' (taken to be Paul Verlaine)

---

3 A. Rimbaud, *Complete Works*, 188, tr. A. Jary.

discussing her 'Infernal Bridegroom' (taken to be Rimbaud). However, before the reader accepts 'Delirium I' as a record of the French poets' famous, gay love affair, it is worth recalling that poetic accounts of people's lives can be distortions, exaggerations, or complete pretense. The reality of the life Verlaine and Rimbaud led may hardly appear in *A Season in Hell*, or in any of Rimbaud's poetry. Poets alter life in their poems as they wish – for artistic reasons, or for any number of motives. It is problematic working back from the poems to the poet's life: this is demonstrated by considering William Shakespeare's *Sonnets* and how they relate to the 'real' Shakespeare's relationship with the beloved youth and the 'Dark Lady', or when considering the 'real' Francesco Petrarch's relationship with the 'real' Laura de Sade, the subject of Petrarch's *Canzoniere*.

Remember, then, that in 'Delirium I: The Foolish Virgin' in *A Season in Hell*, a very clever and self-aware poet (Arthur Rimbaud) is impersonating a strange character called the 'Foolish Virgin' which may relate to Paul Verlaine. Also, if the reader swops the roles of the 'Foolish Virgin' and the 'Infernal Bridegroom', the poem is equally insightful. Even if this is biography or autobiography, it is a very peculiar kind of biography or autobiography. Poems are seldom as straightforward as biographies (or novels) anyway; poems are distinct forms of expression with their own laws and needs. Rimbaud's poems, in particular, are highly idiosyncratic. Given the kind of poet that Rimbaud was, the kind of poems that he wrote, his personal aesthetics, his intense self-awareness (in life as in poetry), and his unique life-philosophy, one should not automatically see texts such as 'Delirium I' as biography.

Paul Verlaine also poeticized Arthur Rimbaud – most famously in poem 'À Arthur Rimbaud':

> Mortel, ange ET démon, autaunt dire Rimbaud,
> Tu mérites la prime place en ce mien livre,
> Bien que tel sot grimaud t'ait traité de ribaud
> Imberbe et de monstre en herbe et de potache ivre.

The poems of Paul Verlaine re-pay any visit, as the poems selected for this book demonstrate. Verlaine is a poet who carved out his own niche in the history of poetry: his poems are instantly recognizable for their imagery and themes, and perhaps for their pure poetic approach, more than anything. Verlaine is a 'poet's poet'.

BIBLIOGRAPHY

BY PAUL VERLAINE

Forty Poems, tr. R. Gant & C. Apcher, Falcon Press, 1948
Œuvres poétiques complètes, ed. Y.-G. Le Dantec, Gallimard, 1951
The Sky Above the Roof, tr. B. Hill, Rupert Hart-Davis, 1957
Odeds en Son Honneur Élégies, Librairie Armand Colin, Paris, 1959
Selected Poems, tr. Joanna Richardson, Penguin, London, 1974
Fêtes galantes, ed. Jean Gaudon, Garnier-Flammarion, 1976
Femmes, Hombres, tr. A. Elliot, Anvil Press, London, 1979
One Hundred and One Poems, tr. N. Shapiro, University Press, Chicago, IL, 1999

ABOUT PAUL VERLANIE

E. Delahaye. *Rimbaud*, Messein, 1928
— . *Souveniers familiers à propos de Rimbaud, Verlaine et Germain Nouveau*, Messein, 1925
W. Fowlie. *Rimbaud*, University of Chicago Press, Chicago, 1965
— . *Rimbaud and Jim Morrison: The Rebel as Poet*, Souvenir, 1995
C.A. Hackett. *Rimbaud*, Hilary House, New York, NY, 1977
— . "Verlaine's Influence on Rimbaud", in Lloyd James Austin, ed. *Studies in Modern French Literature Presented to P. Mansell Jones*, Manchester University Press, Manchester, 1961, 163-180
J. & V. Hanson. *Verlaine, Prince of Poets*, Chatto & Windus, London, 1959
Mario Praz: *The Romantic Agony,* tr. A. Davidson, Oxford University Press, Oxford, 1933
Joanna Richardson. *Verlaine*, Weidenfeld & Nicolson, London, 1971
P. Schmidt. "Visions of Violence: Rimbaud and Verlaine", in G. Stambolian,

228-242

George Stambolian & Elaine Marks, eds. *Homosexuality and French Literature: Cultural Contexts/ Critical Texts*, Cornell University Press, Ithaca, 1979

V.P. Underwood. *Verlaine et l'Angleterre*, Nizet, 1956

BY ARTHUR RIMBAUD

Œuvres, ed. Suzanne Bernard & André Guyaux, Garnier, 1981

Œuvres complètes, ed. Antoine Adam, Gallimard, 1972

Complete Works, Selected Letters, tr. Wallace Fowlie, University of Chicago Press, Chicago, 1966

Collected Poems, ed. Oliver Bernhard, Penguin, London, 1986

Illuminations, tr. Louise Varèse, New Directions, New York, NY, 1946

A Season In Hell, tr. Andrew Jary, Crescent Moon, 2007

Morning of Ecstasy: Selected Poems, tr. Andrew Jary, Crescent Moon, 2007

Life, Life
Selected Poems

Arseny Tarkovsky

translated and edited by Virginia Rounding

Arseny Tarkovsky is the neglected Russian poet, father of the acclaimed film director Andrei Tarkovsky. This new book gathers together many of Tarkovsky's most lyrical and heartfelt poems, in Rounding's clear, new translations. Many of Tarkovsky's poems appeared in his son's films, such as *Mirror, Stalker, Nostalghia and The Sacrifice*. There is an introduction by Rounding, and a bibliography of both Arseny and Andrei Tarkovsky.

Bibliography and notes 124pp 3rd ed   ISBN 9781861712660 Hbk   ISBN 9781861711144

Beauties, Beasts, and Enchantment

CLASSIC FRENCH FAIRY TALES

Translated and with an Introduction
by Jack Zipes

A collection of 36 classic French fairy tales translated by renowned writer Jack Zipes.
Cinderella, *Beauty and the Beast*, *Sleeping Beauty* and *Little Red Riding Hood* are among the
classic fairy tales in this amazing book.
Includes illustrations from fairy tale collections.
Jack Zipes has written and published widely on fairy tales.

'Terrific... a succulent array of 17th and 18th century 'salon' fairy tales'
- *The New York Times Book Review*

'These tales are adventurous, thrilling in a way fairy tales are meant to be... The translation
from the French is modern, happily free of archaic and hyperbolic language... a fine and
sophisticated collection' - *New York Tribune*

'Enjoyable to read... a unique collection of French regional folklore' - *Library Journal*

'Charming stories accompanied by attractive pen-and-ink drawings' - *Chattanooga Times*

Introduction and illustrations   612pp.   ISBN 9781861712510 Pbk   ISBN 9781861713193 Hbk

In the Dim Void

Samuel Beckett's Late Trilogy:
Company, Ill Seen, Ill Said and *Worstward Ho*

by Gregory Johns

This book discusses the luminous beauty and dense, rigorous poetry of Samuel Beckett's late works, *Company, Ill Seen, Ill Said* and *Worstward Ho*. Gregory Johns looks back over Beckett's long writing career, charting the development from the *Molloy-Malone Dies-Unnamable* trilogy through the 'fizzles' of the 1960s to the elegiac lyricism of the *Company* series. Johns compares the trilogy with late plays such as *Ghosts, Footfalls* and *Rockaby*.

Bibliography, notes. Illustrated. 120pp
ISBN 9781861712974 Pbk and ISBN 9781861712608 Hbk
9781861713407 E-book

CRESCENT MOON PUBLISHING

web: www.crmoon.com e-mail: cresmopub@yahoo.co.uk

ARTS, PAINTING, SCULPTURE

The Art of Andy Goldsworthy
Andy Goldsworthy: Touching Nature
Andy Goldsworthy in Close-Up
Andy Goldsworthy: Pocket Guide
Andy Goldsworthy In America
Land Art: A Complete Guide
The Art of Richard Long
Richard Long: Pocket Guide
Land Art In the UK
Land Art in Close-Up
Land Art In the U.S.A.
Land Art: Pocket Guide
Installation Art in Close-Up
Minimal Art and Artists In the 1960s and After
Colourfield Painting
Land Art DVD, TV documentary
Andy Goldsworthy DVD, TV documentary
The Erotic Object: Sexuality in Sculpture From Prehistory to the Present Day
Sex in Art: Pornography and Pleasure in Painting and Sculpture
Postwar Art
Sacred Gardens: The Garden in Myth, Religion and Art
Glorification: Religious Abstraction in Renaissance and 20th Century Art
Early Netherlandish Painting
Leonardo da Vinci
Piero della Francesca
Giovanni Bellini
Fra Angelico: Art and Religion in the Renaissance
Mark Rothko: The Art of Transcendence
Frank Stella: American Abstract Artist
Jasper Johns
Brice Marden
Alison Wilding: The Embrace of Sculpture
Vincent van Gogh: Visionary Landscapes
Eric Gill: Nuptials of God
Constantin Brancusi: Sculpting the Essence of Things
Max Beckmann
Caravaggio
Gustave Moreau
Egon Schiele: Sex and Death In Purple Stockings
Delizioso Fotografico Fervore: Works In Process 1
Sacro Cuore: Works In Process 2
The Light Eternal: J.M.W. Turner
The Madonna Glorified: Karen Arthurs

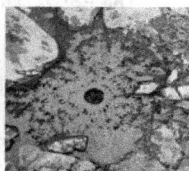

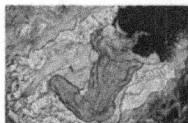

LITERATURE

J.R.R. Tolkien: The Books, The Films, The Whole Cultural Phenomenon
J.R.R. Tolkien: Pocket Guide
Tolkien's Heroic Quest
The *Earthsea* Books of Ursula Le Guin
Beauties, Beasts and Enchantment: Classic French Fairy Tales
German Popular Stories by the Brothers Grimm
Philip Pullman and *His Dark Materials*
Sexing Hardy: Thomas Hardy and Feminism
Thomas Hardy's *Tess of the d'Urbervilles*
Thomas Hardy's *Jude the Obscure*
Thomas Hardy: The Tragic Novels
Love and Tragedy: Thomas Hardy
The Poetry of Landscape in Hardy
Wessex Revisited: Thomas Hardy and John Cowper Powys
Wolfgang Iser: Essays and Interviews
Petrarch, Dante and the Troubadours
Maurice Sendak and the Art of Children's Book Illustration
Andrea Dworkin
Cixous, Irigaray, Kristeva: The *Jouissance* of French Feminism
Julia Kristeva: Art, Love, Melancholy, Philosophy, Semiotics and Psychoanalysis
Hélene Cixous I Love You: The *Jouissance* of Writing
Luce Irigaray: Lips, Kissing, and the Politics of Sexual Difference
Peter Redgrove: Here Comes the Flood
Peter Redgrove: Sex-Magic-Poetry-Cornwall
Lawrence Durrell: Between Love and Death, East and West
Love, Culture & Poetry: Lawrence Durrell
Cavafy: Anatomy of a Soul
German Romantic Poetry: Goethe, Novalis, Heine, Hölderlin
Feminism and Shakespeare
Shakespeare: Love, Poetry & Magic
The Passion of D.H. Lawrence
D.H. Lawrence: Symbolic Landscapes
D.H. Lawrence: Infinite Sensual Violence
Rimbaud: Arthur Rimbaud and the Magic of Poetry
The Ecstasies of John Cowper Powys
Sensualism and Mythology: The Wessex Novels of John Cowper Powys
Amorous Life: John Cowper Powys and the Manifestation of Affectivity (H.W. Fawkner)
Postmodern Powys: New Essays on John Cowper Powys (Joe Boulter)
Rethinking Powys: Critical Essays on John Cowper Powys
Paul Bowles & Bernardo Bertolucci
Rainer Maria Rilke
Joseph Conrad: *Heart of Darkness*
In the Dim Void: Samuel Beckett
Samuel Beckett Goes into the Silence
André Gide: Fiction and Fervour
Jackie Collins and the Blockbuster Novel
Blinded By Her Light: The Love-Poetry of Robert Graves
The Passion of Colours: Travels In Mediterranean Lands
Poetic Forms

POETRY

Ursula Le Guin: Walking In Cornwall
Peter Redgrove: Here Comes The Flood
Peter Redgrove: Sex-Magic-Poetry-Cornwall
Dante: Selections From the Vita Nuova
Petrarch, Dante and the Troubadours
William Shakespeare: Sonnets
William Shakespeare: Complete Poems
Blinded By Her Light: The Love-Poetry of Robert Graves
Emily Dickinson: Selected Poems
Emily Brontë: Poems
Thomas Hardy: Selected Poems
Percy Bysshe Shelley: Poems
John Keats: Selected Poems
Joh n Keats: Poems of 1820
D.H. Lawrence: Selected Poems
Edmund Spenser: Poems
Edmund Spenser: Amoretti
John Donne: Poems
Henry Vaughan: Poems
Sir Thomas Wyatt: Poems
Robert Herrick: Selected Poems
Rilke: Space, Essence and Angels in the Poetry of Rainer Maria Rilke
Rainer Maria Rilke: Selected Poems
Friedrich Hölderlin: Selected Poems
Arseny Tarkovsky: Selected Poems
Arthur Rimbaud: Selected Poems
Arthur Rimbaud: A Season in Hell
Arthur Rimbaud and the Magic of Poetry
Novalis: Hymns To the Night
German Romantic Poetry
Paul Verlaine: Selected Poems
Elizaethan Sonnet Cycles
D.J. Enright: By-Blows
Jeremy Reed: Brigitte's Blue Heart
Jeremy Reed: Claudia Schiffer's Red Shoes
Gorgeous Little Orpheus
Radiance: New Poems
Crescent Moon Book of Nature Poetry
Crescent Moon Book of Love Poetry
Crescent Moon Book of Mystical Poetry
Crescent Moon Book of Elizabethan Love Poetry
Crescent Moon Book of Metaphysical Poetry
Crescent Moon Book of Romantic Poetry
Pagan America: New American Poetry

MEDIA, CINEMA, FEMINISM and CULTURAL STUDIES

J.R.R. Tolkien: The Books, The Films, The Whole Cultural Phenomenon
J.R.R. Tolkien: Pocket Guide
The *Lord of the Rings* Movies: Pocket Guide
The Cinema of Hayao Miyazaki
Hayao Miyazaki: *Princess Mononoke*: Pocket Movie Guide
Hayao Miyazaki: *Spirited Away*: Pocket Movie Guide
Tim Burton : Hallowe'en For Hollywood
Ken Russell
Ken Russell: *Tommy*: Pocket Movie Guide
The Ghost Dance: The Origins of Religion
The Peyote Cult
Cixous, Irigaray, Kristeva: The *Jouissance* of French Feminism
Julia Kristeva: Art, Love, Melancholy, Philosophy, Semiotics and Psychoanalysis
Luce Irigaray: Lips, Kissing, and the Politics of Sexual Difference
Hélene Cixous I Love You: The *Jouissance* of Writing
Andrea Dworkin
'Cosmo Woman': The World of Women's Magazines
Women in Pop Music
HomeGround: The Kate Bush Anthology
Discovering the Goddess (Geoffrey Ashe)
The Poetry of Cinema
The Sacred Cinema of Andrei Tarkovsky
Andrei Tarkovsky: Pocket Guide
Andrei Tarkovsky: *Mirror*: Pocket Movie Guide
Andrei Tarkovsky: *The Sacrifice*: Pocket Movie Guide
Walerian Borowczyk: Cinema of Erotic Dreams
Jean-Luc Godard: The Passion of Cinema
Jean-Luc Godard: *Hail Mary*: Pocket Movie Guide
Jean-Luc Godard: *Contempt*: Pocket Movie Guide
Jean-Luc Godard: *Pierrot le Fou*: Pocket Movie Guide
John Hughes and Eighties Cinema
Ferris Bueller's Day Off: Pocket Movie Guide
Jean-Luc Godard: Pocket Guide
The Cinema of Richard Linklater
Liv Tyler: Star In Ascendance
Blade Runner and the Films of Philip K. Dick
Paul Bowles and Bernardo Bertolucci
Media Hell: Radio, TV and the Press
An Open Letter to the BBC
Detonation Britain: Nuclear War in the UK
Feminism and Shakespeare
Wild Zones: Pornography, Art and Feminism
Sex in Art: Pornography and Pleasure in Painting and Sculpture
Sexing Hardy: Thomas Hardy and Feminism

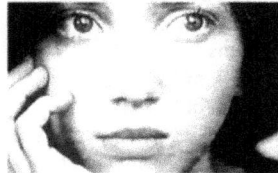

The Light Eternal is a model monograph, an exemplary job. The subject matter of the book is beautifully
organised and dead on beam. (Lawrence Durrell)
It is amazing for me to see my work treated with such passion and respect. (Andrea Dworkin)

CRESCENT MOON PUBLISHING
P.O. Box 1312, Maidstone, Kent, ME14 5XU, Great Britain. www.crmoon.com

cresmopub@yahoo.co.uk   www.crescentmoon.org.uk

www.ingramcontent.com/pod-product-compliance
Lightning Source LLC
Chambersburg PA
CBHW060037050426
42448CB00012B/3051